All Space Away and In

All Space
Away and In

Mark Goodwin

Shearsman Books

First published in the United Kingdom in 2017 by
Shearsman Books
50 Westons Hill Drive
Emersons Green
BRISTOL
BS16 7DF

Shearsman Books Ltd Registered Office
30–31 St. James Place, Mangotsfield, Bristol BS16 9JB
(this address not for correspondence)

www.shearsman.com

ISBN 978-1-84861-563-2

ACKNOWLEDGEMENTS

The poems in this collection, or versions of, have been previously
published by the following, to whose editors I am grateful: *Crystal Clear
Creators, The Interpreter's House, Poetry Wales, Shearsman magazine.*
A sound-enhanced version of 'Imminence East of Westbury' was
exhibited by Creative Wiltshire, as part of Walking Wiltshire White
Horses (2013).

My thanks to the following, for their critical comments and/or encour-
agement relating to individual poems in this collection: Nick Bullock,
David Caddy, Claire Jane Carter, Rob Cooper, Joanna Croston, Harry
Guest, Rob Hamberger, Paul Ings, Chris Jones, Brian Lewis, Charles
Lauder, Robert Macfarlane, Martin Malone, Helen Mort, Stuart
Mugridge, Jim Perrin, Zoë Skoulding, Maria Taylor, Julia Thornley.

Thank you to Nia Davies –
for her vital critical comments on 'Gulls & Jacks'.

Thank you to my partner Nikki Clayton –
for her photo that covers *All Space Away and In*,
and for her company in all those spaces … in … and away …

Contents

for Julia

Gleam-Form at Resipole, December 2011

sudden cloud-slot slides

                                     inland up off

sea blue-black sky split

                 by bright

sun clips

         hill-ridge fractures

                      glow across

Loch Sun Art's pelt

       lit ripples collect

                               otter-shape

long whisker

             -wake arrowing

from round snout now a

                 gloss-otter's

tapered snake of tale slides

                      gone   cloudsclose

Cove & Machinery, a Loch Warren, a Pembroke

below gorse grass & thrift
below spring's blaze
of smells & sun-fed

colours below
coast-path lip

a carpark-wide expanse of

                                                            stone-
sheet slant

                        hairline-crack crissed
                rippled gun-greys & rusts
        rock-scurf splinters
wind can lift

                                                            epoch-
tilted

at base sea's erosion-swirl-white
                -frilling now's passing layers

we balance down the slab on elephant skin
                finger-widths of cardboard-box-thick
        square-edge flakes clink & scrape

                        geology-fragrance & sea's forever-
rhythm

at bottom amongst
sea-greened-&-blackened boulders

some ship's bent engine block
with big . pebbles . hammered
fast into its . slots . clamped
to . gether . steel&stonetight
as . horizon . squashed bysky

we

                                                        look up

high on a friable face
                of zag-zig rifts
a stone

                                                        -tock a
rock-

clunk-&-puff-of-dirt-&-now-rattle of
                some small falling portion

of land's rind

Forming Off A Dinas Fawr,
A Pembroke, An Easter 2011

a Milford Haven's oil-spires prong up
from a dark band of land across St Bride's Bay

       we sit at a tip of a Dinas Fawr's jut
       on wiry coast grass in sunlight slid
                   on wind

            we cannot hear ocean rumbling over
                  a lip of a world's
end

       a half-mile off land
       a squadron of white crosses
       black-tipped spearhead-wings

          circle-soaring where sky
          hangs its vast hollow over ocean

a——Skomer——Island's——dark——slice—— hangs——on——horizon

      one bright-white cross
              stalls

                now two now three
                  arrow-folds
fall

               to white-flash per

     cussion
     bombs on
      sea

ten or more miles   away a black tanker   falls off Earth's boiling edge

    seconds on

laser-white
  -foam-smudges-
flap-up-

     gannet-formed

Orca, Solfach Uchaf, Pembroke

twilight glanced off sea

a wooden five-bar gate back
-lit by skyfoil a big

                                        badger slips his

black-grey-white-stripe-shape through
            a gap between
sea-sky-ground & bottom rail his

quick cross glare at
                   us is hot his eyes
twilight-precise his
                      paws thump earth a

dark drystone-dyke-hole nettle-frilled
            swallows

                                      an elongation of his speed

Gulls & Jacks, A Gower, A July 2013

jackdaws' *jack* calls bounce

off seagulls' shiny scree

                            ches we

        perch

        on a point on

        earth a

limestone promontory holds
our positions

                high

above a bowl of ground balanced

on an im

                agined's edge as

                                ocean's

capillaries & veins
entangle and

        release sizzling   (as
        a vast's cilia in

        ter- & un-

        lock with
        solid's brink   ) as

                    sea feels

with mineral
-thick liquid feels

into a shore's

                micro

-fractal pock
ets & chambers a   far

                                        star zaps

limestone explosion-bright and

            heats

air to bend as
breeze

            it seems

barely cools fusion's force to

                    day

sea is sheer
smooth to

horizon where

                        Lundy hangs

like a Buddhist carp or
some expedition space

                                        -ship just

                                        beyond some far

                                        flung world's

                                        biosphere round

a cliff-rimmed bowl
seagulls dive and

            slide

                        and they

they have shadows
                        shadows

rippling along ground
                        changing

ground's colours   darkening
grass- & -fern-greens   deepening

            sea-pinks and   leaving

                        moments

of print-black
shooting shapes like

some alphabet's time

                        -lapsed
                                    evolution and

the jackdaws too have

                    shadows
                    shadows

white as chalk or

neon-white as
sun snags

                                        a wing

-edge or flash
-splashes glas

                    sy breast feathers

jacks have gulls
                                for white

            doubles

and now
            now one

one gull's gr
                        ounded shadow

-double zooms huge

            and tiny and huge and

                                    small as

its projected form follows
a crag's

                ins

            & outs

Imminence East of Westbury

to East high-horse
thunder-heads

bubble up chalkily

air's still
ness sudd

enly swaps
to gusts

a sultry August
day's soul is

going

to kick

kick its door down
kick a sky open it's

going to

go

going to bolt and
be gone

a day's compressed

hot chalky
solidity is

reaching

critical mass   snorts
chalk breaths

chalk anvils blackening
at back as

thunder builds

chalk-hooves flint-ringing
cloud galloping

electricity's jagged
stallion-hairs craze

a white-glare crackling flag

chalk's pale
sound wobbles

cold as neon

a pole of light
plants its

milliseconds of seed
beneath grass

ground rip

ples like a horse's
fly-irritated hide

a high
pitched

ice-bright

miles long string
of chalky whinny

homes in

instantly all
bones glint and

ring

Ptarmigan Mist, Am Bodach, March 2016

Note: *Am Bodach* is a mountain just north of the head of Loch Leven, its name means – *The Old Man*

behind us is
sunlit snow

& soft white blades
of corniced ridges

& Am Bodach's
black rocks set

in shining névé

parts of our
minds are

behind us on
Am Bodach's

summit at a

recent past set
in a glistening

history of

lit minutes & iced
metres we have

just traversed

at summit fog
enfolded ground

and we descended

through grey air

on mist-smudged snow
and just to our

north the faint

dangerous line where
sky & cornice merge

and to south
clear black rocks

of safe solidity
up-poked and

marked way

now here in

a fog-hollow of
corrie in

front of
us perched on

a snow-tussock
a ptarmigan

bold & gazing
caped in white

red-smudged black
-slash eye-mask

hooked apple-pip beak
thick frosted legs

his

sudden ratchety
guttural call a

miniature thunder

he is

massive in his
little proudness

a bird of
mountain

his feathery
snow slopes his
crag-black rudder

his cornice-grace
ful curves

in front of us
now a mountain
of bird

set in mist pulls
Am Bodach's

mass and we
are tiny figures

climbing along a
ptarmigan's wing

As Fish Nudge Circles,
an Ogwen, a Snowdonia, an August 2012

for Louis & Nikki

we scrambled rhyolite whilst
flying-ants drank
our sweat

or at least it felt
like that as they
clung to us

those in the air
dark spark
-like filaments frenzied
with lust

black flakes thick
as blizzard
haloed Eve & Adam

as I climbed Adam
I had to sweep
holds free of ants

Eve's stony skin
had become
wriggling black fur
jewelled with gleam

ing cellophane wings and

as I jumped the gap
I wondered if I'd

skid on insects

black flecks plast
ered my face as
I passed through
a cloud of

fibrous beings
their wings' quick
ratchety-pitch itch
ing in my ears as

a strange wiry choir
entered my brain

after Tradition's jump
I posed for a photo
my hair alive
with crawling angels
my nape dark
as Velcro tickling but

not one
insect bit me

      *

      last time here
      on Tryfan's summit

      for this jump between
      these petrified sinners

      (that I failed to make)

      February frost had

feathered their skins

and the air hummed
whirling fractured zeros

speck-sized oms cold
as white-hot pins

pricked my skin

dots & flecks
of white Velcro

snagged on my whiskers

*

sudden solid sound a

jet-fighter blast follow
ing a camouflaged arrowhead

below us distinctly blurred

an angular detached
hi-tech patch
of ground hurtled

down Ogwen and banked
at the valley-bend tugging out

of us our
gasps as

its boom bounced off

Y Garn & Foel-goch

*

now Tryfan's rugged yet
delicate mosaic of time-

-&-weather-embroidered-
        blocks-slabs-spikes-
    flakes-&-pinnacles is
fragments of memory behind us

we descend from the bwlch
salt in our eyes
our feet hot and tightly-socked
sweating in mountain-boots

it's six o' clock and
the August sun
still has power in it

(most of the ants've
been brushed off just
a few remains crushed
under our rucksack straps

perhaps an odd stray
still alive trapped
in hair or rucked cloth)

*

suddenly Cwm Bochlwyd
becomes a rumbling

bowl of Welsh syllables

shepherds' commands bounce
off Glyder Fach

but we see no one

a hundred or so
metres below us
Llyn Bochlwyd's cool

glitter pulls
pulls us towards to
wards its smooth

silent finite dialogue
with vast sky whilst

a man cross

with his dog
spreads his voice
around the cwm

vivid voice like

smoke blown
through water hangs

on the crags and colours

the air

*

peace-&-glee-blend-as
the llyn's sheen illumin
ates our faces

momentarily each wear
masks of jangling light

our feet freezing
deliciously in blade-clear

                              llyn-water   fish

                              nudge circles in
                              to expanding
                              existences and yet

men & beasts are at
work noisily

                *

there are three
shepherds yelling

one of them like song
soft yodelling paid
out across distance in
to his dog's ears

another's is harsh
guttural rocks hurled
across a cwm's void

at a bad dog

another detonates cutting *coos*
and barks *yaaahs* to clear
the cwm of straying sheep

clear ringing whistles whip
out directional instruction

and still we see no

*

one   but across valley high
on a ragged crag-edge

six small creamy
balls roll a
part as a black
dart of dog bursts
their flock   a scream

of Welsh rises to
wards the young mutt

I imagine a mix of
commands & insults &
a flux of Welsh-&-English

can't be certain but
that just sounded like

you fucking cunt

the errant collie
a black splinter falling
down hillside following

an ant's-egg-sized
ewe towards

cliff-edge yaps as
the shepherd's
throat thrusts

heavy-hard-glass-sharp-words

surely the ewe will fall
now to her death down
the crag floating like

a skin-flake or
brushed-off
pill of lint but

                              no

she stops and
resists the dark
pointed jab
of the dog

right on the lip
the shepherd's voice
by-now gone
supersonic hits his

dog spot-on and pulls

it off and back
up hill   his
commands now

lodging in the dog's mind

Electric

my boy & I swim
in my dad's lake

today the lake is crinkled slate
a liquid rattling of dark
corrugation pressed

by a bulbous evolving sky

                    thunder's sub

stance inflates space & colours and

        yet

its vast hollow thuds prick pin

-point sharp where

                    we are

my boy's eyes spark
with controlled terror

and free amazement

back-dropped by
pumped-up purple
the tall willows are
metallic-green and vibrate as

air begins and

        ends on

each fish-shaped leaf

wind peels off
      faint but crisp
            layers of light
                  grey lake-spray

my boy & I hang
in undulating water   we
scrunch our eyes as

              suddenly hail

pixelates our faces
the lake's pocked wrig

                gling skin sizzles

my boy's rapturous voice blurs
with a world's ringing
layers and my

            voice joins his

a dripping crow hunkers
in the lantern of the young
sycamore by the stile

a startled moorhen drags
her fast trail of watery arrows
into the reeds' *shrish*

shelter for our bodies
is a whole house

      of lake

my boy & I are two heads
poked into air's storm bobbing
on a trembling membrane as

        our bodies hang

swayed in the lake's first
moments of depth quiet

below us where

      fish wait in soft silts

              above us

sky's miles rise
through electric clouds

suddenly light

        ening takes

all space away and in
stantly gives

      back all time as

          A

         single place

               etched-in-flash

my boy & I laugh and

laugh a life

    time's

        glee-&-fright